THE PREACHER
AND HIS SERMON

REV. J. PATERSON SMYTH

By Rev. J. PATERSON SMYTH,

B.D., LL.D., LITT.D., D.C.L.

THE PREACHER
AND HIS SERMON

BY

REV. J. PATERSON SMYTH,
B.D., LL.D., LITT.D., D.C.L.
LATE PROFESSOR OF PASTORAL THEOLOGY, UNIVERSITY OF DUBLIN

*Author of "A People's Life of Christ," "Story of St. Paul's
Life and Letters," "The Gospel of the Hereafter,"
"The Bible in the Making," etc.*

NEW YORK
GEORGE H. DORAN COMPANY

THE PREACHER AND HIS SERMON. I
PRINTED IN THE UNITED STATES OF AMERICA

Addressed to Divinity Students and Junior Clergy in the University of Trinity College, Dublin, and later in Trinity University, Toronto.

CONTENTS

Lecture I
THE PREACHER

THE PREACHER

§ 1

THE subject to be dealt with is "The Preacher and his Sermon." I want to do all that in me lies to help you to be good preachers and to preach good sermons. It is a comfort to think that this does not necessitate that I should be a good preacher myself and preach good sermons. It only needs that I should be trying hard to be and do such in so far as my own personal limitations permit. Some of us can never be what would be considered very good preachers. But any poor struggler after excellence who for more than twenty years has himself been honestly trying hard to learn how to preach should be able to help you to preach. He can tell you of the faults that have been spoiling his own preaching, and of his efforts to discover and correct them; of the methods that he has tried and found wanting or found useful; of the things that have helped him and hindered him. He can tell you all that he has gathered from other men's experience. Above all, he can tell you, for your encouragement, of his continually growing interest and enthusiasm in his preaching, that makes him able to-day to say to you in all sincerity that he would not change his office for that of a king. Therefore, you must not think it at all presumption that a man who is very much dissatisfied with his own preaching should venture to occupy this chair and teach you how to preach.

I ask your careful attention to the title of these addresses, "The Preacher and His Sermon." The preacher first—the man first. That is a thought which I desire to impress deeply upon you, that in the ministerial life it is not so much the doing of the duties that is important as the kind of man who is doing the duties; it is not so much the sort of sermon that is preached as the sort of man that is behind the sermon. I think that was the thought in St. Paul's mind when advising the young minister Timothy, "Take heed to thyself and to thy teaching"—*thyself first*.

Looking back on my experience of men I see more and more the need of emphasising this, that the personality of the preacher is of supreme importance. Preaching has been well defined as the communication of truth *by man to men, i.e.,* the bringing of truth to men through a human personality.[1] So you see there are the *two* elements, the truth of God *and* the personality of the preacher. Both count. The personality of the most sympathetic preacher will not help men much unless it has the truth of God behind it; but, on the other hand, it would seem that the truth of God to be fully effective needs to be brought to men through the heart of a sympathetic man. This latter is what most needs emphasising for you young men. You realise at once that the truth matters much. It is not so easy to realise that you yourself matter much, yet that is what you must realise if ever you are to be a true preacher. I do believe that what God is especially seeking for the ministry to-day, is men who are capable of being vehicles of His truth to humanity; men who are open on the Godward side to receive divine impressions, to feel divine cravings, to thrill with divine enthusiasm, and who are open on the manward side to have that sympathy and touch with their

[1] Phillips Brooks.

poor struggling brethren which make the truth
which passes through them electric and attractive. It is only in proportion as a man is thus
qualified that he can ever become in any real
sense a preacher of righteousness; a prophet
of the Lord God. There will be fifty preachers
in our city pulpits next Sunday, preaching in
the main the same truths, and yet with such a
difference. One will emphasise a side of truth
that does not occur at all to another; one will
put a thing dully and uninterestingly, another
will make it so vivid that he will force you to
see it; one will preach a sermon as clear as crys-
tal, but as cold, too—you will feel that the truth
he is teaching has never touched his heart; another will carry you with him in spite of yourself, and will thrill you with the deep feeling
that his subject has roused in himself. The
difference is in the personality of the men:
partly the difference of natural manner and
temperament which makes one personality more
attractive than another; chiefly the difference of
depth of character and devotional life, which
makes one man so much more sensitive than
another to the divine influences above him and
to the human influences around him.

I think I shall the better help you to feel the

importance of the personal element if I remind you of the way in which God inspired the Bible. He might have spoken His revelation daily direct from Heaven; or written it across the sky, or branded it for ever on the everlasting hills; there it would be permanently before men, and with the great advantage of being God's direct infallible word, not passed through any distorting or fallible medium. But God did not do that, surely because that was not the best way to influence men. Instead of giving a ready-made revelation sent down from Heaven He passed His truth through human hearts and minds, He inspired poor stupid fallible human beings who could easily make mistakes; who could but imperfectly grasp His teaching. He inspired them with noble thoughts and high enthusiasms, and restless cravings and longings after Himself; He kept their souls open and receptive, that His teaching might be received by them; He kept them in sympathetic touch with their brethren that they might be the fitter to communicate to them His comfort and help. They were on the one side receiving from God, they were on the other communicating to men; they imparted to men their hopes and enthusiasms and the knowledge that God had conveyed to their souls. They did it, doubtless, very imperfectly, and yet they did it humanly, and so they were able to influence humanity around them. It would seem that in God's sight it was worth risking some error and imperfection that His truth might come to men warm from human hearts like their own. And it would seem that different types of men were needed to present different sides of truth. God used the men best fitted for each country and each age. He inspired various characters and temperaments. He chose men of different tones of thought to present the different aspects of His many-sided truths, and thus to correct and supplement each other. So, too, that Divine Spirit touched men at various crises in their lives, surely in order that the various notes might be struck in the harmony of God's revelation. He came to them in joy, in sorrow, in doubt, in despair, in the glad confidence of faith, in the fierce struggle with temptation. Through the human spirit in its various states He spake to the universal human spirit as it could never have been spoken to otherwise. He spake through the passionate indignation of Isaiah, and the sorrowful plaints of Jeremiah, over the wickedness of his race. He touched the hearts of the ancient Psalmists in their various life crises, and we hear their struggle with their sorrow and their sin, and their childlike crying after the living God. He inspired the stern pathos of Hosea, sorrowing over the greatest trouble that could come to man, a wife unfaithful to her marriage vow, and by means of his sorrow and his changeless love, learning Jehovah's feelings towards His unfaithful people.

That is how God inspired and trained the writers of the Bible, *and that is how He will inspire and train each one of you* who is fit for His high office, fit to be a prophet of the Lord Jehovah. Do not take this as unreal talk. God is really training His preachers to-day as He trained them in ancient days. Some of us older men know in our own keen experience that it is so. My young brothers, as I look into your faces to-day and think how God is going to train you for your future ministry, it is to me very pathetic. I look back to my own student days and think of the experience through which God has since been training me. I think of the dear loving old rector, who helped me by his faith in God, and the kindly blunt people in my first parish from whom I learned so much.

I think of the deep happiness of my home, and the little children clinging to me to teach me what is the great central truth of my life, the deep tenderness of God's fatherhood. I think of many months of illness and pain, to teach me sympathy with the suffering. I think of one very dear to me passing suddenly into the Unseen, and forcing my heart after him to grope at the doors of that Wondrous Life, where he had gone in. I think of many such things in God's training of myself, and as I ask my brother clergy I find similar things true of them. And, therefore, I say to you, it is very pathetic, but it is absolutely true that God will train every man of you who is worth the training as He trained the inspired teachers of old.

My young brethren, if this that I say to you be true—and you know in your hearts that it is, even if you have never thought about it before—if it be true, I say, should it not bring a deep solemnity into our thoughts about preaching? Surely it must make you feel that to be a true preacher means much more than to learn tricks of manner and gesture, and rules about the logical composition of sermons—that all the teaching of the Divinity School, and all the gathered experience of other men can contribute but a small element to the making of a preacher. That to make a true real preacher requires first of all, as a foundation, to make a true real man.

§ 2

If I am right in all this that I have said about the importance of *yourself,* of the personal element in you as a preacher, two things would seem to follow—

(1) That you must always try only to be *yourself,* your own natural self.

(2) That you must try to be your *very best self,* the very best self that you are capable of being.

1st. That you must be your own self, not try to be an imitator of somebody else. You will sometimes be tempted, when you see or read the work of stronger and better and abler men than yourself, to think that if you could preach as they preach, or put things in their way, or imitate in some degree their manners or gesture, you would gain in efficiency. I do not think so at all. You had much better try to remain always your own natural self, to live the special life which God has marked out for you, and which He has indicated by the special powers and the special temperament and characteristics which you find in yourself. It is a mysterious thing this personality of ours. God has sent us into the world each with his own distinct personality, as with his own distinct features or handwriting. We have each his own individual temperament and capacities and talents and sympathies, each his own way of thinking and looking at things. My way of looking at or putting a truth is not exactly your way; your way is not exactly that of the man beside you on these benches. As God has given to every seed his own body, to every flower his own form, so has He laid down to every human being an order according to which it is natural that he should develop, and it is in his developing according to this order that he can best discharge his duty and deliver a true message to men. I think it was of special purpose that God chose all the different personalities of the men who should be inspired to give His revelation to the world; and I think it is of set purpose that God calls you with your different personalities. You will each do best as you are, not as a copy of some one else. Your individuality is a sacred thing and comes into God's plan for you; therefore, emphatically I repeat,

"Be yourself." Never try to imitate greater men than yourself, except in this one thing, trying to be as true and noble and self-forgetting and devoted to God as you believe they are.

Be yourself! your natural self! That is the way to become original preachers in the true, right sense of the word. There is a great desire with young preachers in the beginning of their ministry to be original; they hate to be considered as preaching commonplace truths, or saying things just in the same way as everybody else. They like to be thought in some way original, out of the common, expressing thoughts peculiar to themselves. Sometimes it leads to their being silly and ridiculous. But it need not, and it ought not. The truth that comes out of your own inner self as part of yourself should be for that reason in some sense original and peculiar to you. If you want to be an original preacher, let the truth you teach be so assimilated that it has become *part of yourself*. Look at Heaven and hell and sin and holiness with your *own* eyes, listen *for yourself* to the voice of God, ask God to reveal to *you* His love, His generosity, the beauty of His character, and then tell men these things just as they appear to you. Get down to the heart of things, get below the surface down to the facts which lie behind all appearances, and talk to men naturally of them as they appear to yourself. That will lead to an originality which will last all your life. Men will be attracted by the personal note which unconsciously runs through your teaching. The thoughts will seem the stronger because you have thought them yourself, the feeling will be more vivid because you have felt it yourself, and they will know that you are a real man speaking to them, trying to lead them to God by a way along which you have gone yourself. *Yourself*. YOURSELF. Give them yourself. Keep yourself very unobtrusive. Except on the very rarest occasions, never talk of yourself. But underneath all the shyness and modesty and unobtrusiveness, let the personal note ring through all you say. Let men feel that it is *your* thought, *your* feeling, *your* hope, *your* craving, *your* enthusiasm. There is a marvellous attractiveness for men in that.

§ 3

But this does not mean that you are to be the crude unfinished imperfect self that you are now. No! Be yourself, but be your *best* self.

22

Be the fullest, noblest self that it is possible for you to be. You must develop on the natural lines that God has laid down for you. But see to it that you *do* develop. You have to develop on many sides.

(1st.) I have pointed out to you that to be a true preacher it is necessary to keep your soul open, facing God, receiving continually from God high impulses, desires, enthusiasms that you are to communicate to men.

Need I repeat to you that that is the supreme element in a successful preacher: successful I mean in drawing men towards God. As you think on all the ministries that you know, and search out what distinguishes the successful from the unsuccessful preacher, you know right well that you have to go deeper than eloquence and cleverness and attractiveness of style, and such external things. You will see men who are very eloquent and very scholarly, and very well equipped with advantages of voice and manner, yet somehow they do not impress you or rouse you to any enthusiasm for righteousness. And some day you come upon a man who seems deficient in most of these things, a poor, awkward, shy man, lacking in method, lacking in manner, lacking in eloquence and cleverness

23

and literary style, and yet you will find the doubter, and the tempted, and the struggling instinctively turn to him for help. Why? Not because he has been well taught in the Divinity School the external duties of his office. No; but because he is a real man, really praying, really struggling, really trying to live in communion with God.

And then I pointed out to you the correlative of this, the need of keen sympathy with your fellows. You have that also in some degree already, else you would not be longing to help them and lift them upward. But it will greatly develop in your ministry if you are a true kindly man. You must get to know your people intimately, their struggles and wants and sorrows; their hopes and interests and desires and cares. It is in knowing and sympathising deeply with those, and feeling deeply, at the same time, that there is true comfort for their sorrows, and true satisfaction for their cravings in the following of Christ, and only there—it is in this lies the secret of your success as a preacher.

(2nd.) These are the supreme things, the foundation things. But there is much more. When God is sending you on so grand and solemn a mission you must see to it that you fit yourself on all sides. You must see that your voice and your manner of speaking are the best that they can be made. You have opportunities now that our generation had not. I cannot understand any man realising the greatness of his office as a preacher and yet going on with an unpleasant or untrained voice, and a trick of dropping the ends of his sentences, or any other defect that is hindering his effectiveness. I want you not to take for granted that you are all right, that you can read well and speak well. I went on for years without discovering the defects of my utterance, and I am hearing on every side the complaints of the lay people that we clergy, and the younger clergy especially, read so badly and preach so fast that they cannot easily follow them. I have still to keep church-wardens and parishioners listening in awkward corners to tell me when I drop my voice or when I speak too fast. I should strongly advise you to do the same.

And you must read hard. In these days, when every one reads, you will have to read more strenuously and widely and deeply than the laity whom you are to lead. A narrow man, an uncultured man, a man who has not learned to think hard, will be at a great disadvantage. He cannot be a leader. And no matter what people say of the impossibility of our still being leaders of thought in these days of widespread culture, yet leaders of thought we must all aim to be. And leaders of thought in our own special direction we all of us can be. But we must work hard for it.

That is all I have to say to you to-day. Yourself is a supremely important element in your preaching. Therefore aim to be your real self, and not an imitation. Therefore also aim to be your best self—spiritually, intellectually, physically—every way. Make up your mind that if you are an uninteresting preacher, if people don't care to listen to you, it is most probably your own fault. Try to find out if people are listening to you; if you are interesting them, if you are helping them. If not, try to find out the reason and remedy it. Never give up trying. Never give up improving. And above all, never give up hoping and rejoicing and being enthusiastic about your preaching. Do not lose heart because the ideal set before you is high. You have all your life to attain to it. You have all the strength and help of God to enable you to do it. And when you have done your best, for God's sake, not for your own, if you never become a great or interesting or attractive preacher, you have the comfort that no true man is ever a failure in the sight of God. When the great householder in the parable called his servants to their account and their award, when one had gained two talents and another had gained five, His warm, glad, hearty, "Well done," rings out for them both; the warm, hearty appreciation of the Master who loved to praise and hated to blame, who hoped they would succeed and was glad that they should succeed. And He does not say, "Well done, good and successful servant," or good and popular servant—that is not always in a man's power to attain. But "Well done, good and *faithful* servant"—faithful in God's sight, though perhaps a failure in man's —"enter thou into the joy of thy Lord."

THE PREACHER: HIS FIRST FIVE YEARS

LECTURE II

THE PREACHER: HIS FIRST FIVE YEARS

OUR subject to-day is, "The Preacher: His First Five Years." I want to say to you first of all, "Resolve at the very beginning that all your life you will try to put your very best into your Sunday Sermon, that if something has to give way in the rush of your work, it certainly shall not be the Sunday Sermon." One hears silly talk nowadays amongst young clergy that the sermon has lost its power, because the laity are reading so much more widely. Don't you believe it, young men. It will be a fatal thing for the power of the Church if ever the younger clergy begin to think that the sermon need not be taken too seriously. The average listener does not want to be careless and uninterested. The average listener, in spite of all appearances to the contrary, longs to be made to listen, and will listen to you eagerly, attentively, delightedly, if you are a real man, preaching from your heart real truths. The true "Speaking

Man," as Carlyle calls him, can never be superseded nor out of date. "The Speaking Man,"
he says, "has, indeed, in these days wandered
terribly from the point, yet at bottom whom
have we to compare with him? Of all public
functionaries boarded and lodged on the industry of modern Europe, is there one worthier of
his board than he? If he could only not wan-
der from the point! If he could only find the
point again!" Carlyle was right. There is a
power and attraction in the living voice of the
true preacher, which never can be superseded
by any increase of knowledge. In God's name,
therefore, work hard, pray hard, do your best
to become true preachers.

Now for the first five years, the most critical
years of your ministry. I am thinking of my
own first five years, with shame and regret, and
wish that some older clerical friend had ad-
vised me what to preach and what not to preach
in the beginning. I had no idea about it, no
plan. I never knew any month what I might
be likely to preach before the month was over.
It was all chance. I began well enough. I began by preaching much about the love of God.
After a few months of sick visiting and deathbeds in a large artisan parish, it seemed to me

that the people were assuming the love of God a great deal too much already, and that their careless deathbeds arose a good deal from the vague notion that God was so kind and good-natured that life and character did not matter much, that a man need only learn to say on his deathbed, "God be merciful to me a sinner." So I changed my tone and began to frighten them about character-making and probation and eternal justice, as if the Father were like a great police magistrate. It was a pity—it was stupidly done, and badly and falsely. After the first year I worked myself into a great state against Calvinistic teaching, which still existed in that district. It seemed to me a brave and knightly thing, to do battle with what seemed a blasphemous travesty of God. It really was not at all brave and knightly, for Calvinism was fast dying out, and it was easy to throw stones at a dying Creed. But mine was a stage of thought very common to all young clergy who feel strongly and enthusiastically about things, and feel also a little bit conceited as to their mission to set things right. At that stage we greatly enjoy criticising with excessive severity the errors of the traditional theology. We generally exaggerate them a good deal and

33

criticise them unfairly. We generally irritate some of the elder clergy and puzzle some of the elder laity with our crude passionate assaults. But we thoroughly enjoy it, and generally we do it well and interestingly because we feel it strongly. I shall tell you afterwards what I think of the value of such preaching. Then came a stage when I thought I had preached on everything under the sun that was worth preaching about, and I remember how the dear old rector laughed when I told him, before I had been very long ordained, that I did not know of anything else now to preach about. I fear the same thing goes on still, and that your experience will be much the same as mine if I cannot suggest anything to help you.

§ 1

I think in the very beginning of your preaching you had best be let alone to express the thoughts that have been most stirring in you during the years before. Whatever you feel strongly about, whatever has been prominent in your own mind, begin with that, read up about it, broaden your knowledge of it, tell it as earnestly as you can. It may not be very

34

valuable, but it is, for the time, the best you have to say, and what you are likely to say best since you feel it strongly. Besides, it will do you good to clear and crystallise thoughts that have been a bit vague and in solution, as it were, for years before. Say, therefore, at first, what you feel most strongly impelled to say.

Only—and let this word sink down into your hearts—be modest, *modest,* VERY MODEST; especially in your earlier sermons I beseech you to be modest. I have been hearing the lay comments on young clergy at the beginning of their ministry, till the thought has stamped itself on me, that a poor stupid young preacher, if he be very modest, will win the affection and regard of the people, while a really able, thoughtful, scholarly man who gives any hint that he thinks himself so, will get their backs up at once. I have known men whose whole position in their parish was affected by their first sermon. I remember some who began by confidently explaining their duties to men who had been following Christ before the preacher was born. And I remember a sermon by one of my own young curates just ordained who began by preaching about the miracle of the barley loaves; and after pointing out how Christ demands from us whatever poor little thing we have, and then blesses and increases it for the help of others, he closed his sermon by saying, "How else could I dare to appear before you to-day, young, ignorant, stupid, inexperienced, with my poor little miserable barley loaves? Only I am longing and praying that the Lord will do with them as he did of old, and that, perhaps, even by means of me, some one may be helped." That congregation took him to their hearts at once. I trust my warning is not necessary for you. It ought not to be, for any young preacher who realises the tremendous solemnity of his position, and his own unfitness for it, and, I trust, you will realise that.

And there is another warning needed, for a young preacher beginning. Indeed it is but part of the same warning as to modesty. Be careful in your earliest sermons to try and *gain the confidence of the people*. It is not at all difficult, for the congregation is usually disposed to have a kindly sympathetic feeling for a young man beginning. They are kindlier to all of us than we deserve but especially in our young days. A young man modest and earnest and desirous to help them, easily wins their sympathy.

36

If he be anything of a thinker and has strong youthful opinions on certain debated subjects he will like to air those opinions. Better not just yet. If some of the things on which you feel strongly are amongst the burning questions, questions on which there is suspicion or controversy—I think you ought to defer them till the people have got to know you, or at any rate be expressly careful as to the impression you may leave. You have, I hope, learned by this time how very unlikely I am to advise you to be timid preachers, or to hide any of God's truth however distasteful. You must often preach things that are distasteful to people. But it is only commonsense to say, don't begin with what may be distasteful when you have so many other truths to teach. The people who regard youth as likeable do not regard it as infallible. Some of the less educated people especially are at first a bit watchful and suspicious of the younger clergy, just come fresh from the Divinity Schools. I was told, some time since, of an old rector in the country who got a new curate. The new curate was an enthusiast. He made people sit up and listen who were accustomed to be somnolent when the rector preached. One day, the rector asked his churchwarden, "Why do you go to sleep when I preach, and listen so carefully to the sermon of Mr. X——?" "Ah! sir," replied the churchwarden, "we know it is all right when you preach, but we are not so sure about these young curates." We may smile at that feeling. But long experience has taught me to say to you, never despise it, and do not resent it unless you know that it arises from mere desire to find fault. Some of the truest and most earnest Christian men of the less educated classes— men who will be your most faithful helpers— may easily be estranged from you by unnecessary suspicion until they get to know you. Therefore, be careful, and remember it is part of the duty you owe to your parish and to your Lord not to put a stumbling-block before one of His little ones.

§ 2

I told you to begin by saying what you yourself felt most deeply. In a very short time you will have dealt with all such subjects, and will probably begin to wonder, as I did, whether there was anything else in the whole range of truth worth preaching about. There will come to you that miserable experience of wondering every Monday "What on earth am I to preach about next Sunday?" You will probably worry and waste your time over that for most of the week, and then rush to prepare some subject hurriedly for Sunday. This must not go on. ━━ It is not only a waste of time, it is also a severe nerve strain on any earnest man, and will result in very unsatisfactory sermons. Try to be orderly and systematic and calm. Try to plan beforehand for some weeks what you are going to preach about. Try not to fall into the haphazard way of teaching from the pulpit, which is much too common. In some pulpits there is no order, no system. Men dip in here and there into the Bible in the most random way. No one can prepare for their teaching. No one has any idea what it will be about. One day a verse from St. James, then a verse out of the Chronicles, odd verses and odd subjects at random, without any order or connection in the teaching.

Such random haphazard teaching will never help your people to an orderly systematic grasp of religious truth. Of course you must often preach on separate disconnected subjects. But behind them should lie the great basal foundations, the fundamental truths of Christianity.

For 2000 years the church has prescribed a valuable course of teaching in the order of the Christian Year. The Roman and Greek and Anglican churches are bound to this scheme to their great advantage. I think it would be well for preachers in any Christian denomination to follow a plan tested for centuries.

Begin in December with the four Advent Sundays in preparation for Christmas. Teach of the First Coming, the preparation in history for Christ and the Second Coming in so far as you understand it. Then the Christmas Story and the teaching about the Incarnation. A couple of months later comes the six weeks of Lenten teaching before Easter. Preach on Sin, Repentance, Prayer, Bible Study, Holy Communion and the inner devotional life. Easter and the Sundays immediately following give fine opportunities for teaching about the Resurrection and the great Forty Days before the Ascension. These might well be followed by a series on the Life after Death. The Whitsuntide season would of course be occupied with preaching about the Holy Spirit.

Thus you have a series of teaching from December to May on the basal truths of religion. The other half year would remain for

your separate subjects prominent in which
should be events in the Life of Our Lord.

§ 3

This should help you in some degree in your
Monday perplexity. To go further in this direction I would sketch out a few courses of
sermons. The Creed is rather too difficult a
series to begin with. Try an easier course, say
the Parables. They can be made very interesting. By the way, in addition to Trench and
such other books, there is a capital little treatise
by Marcus Dods, full of freshness and new
points of view; I strongly recommend it. Another very simple and interesting series would
be on Bible biographies. In any of these subjects your senior brother clergy could probably
advise you as to books that you did not know
of. For example, in preaching about the men
of the Old Testament, you might begin by reading Stanley's *Jewish Church*. Then Nisbet
and Co., London, have published a series of
monographs on the men of the Bible. There is
a book of lectures by Fredk. Denison Maurice
on the *Patriarchs and Lawgivers,* also on the
Prophets and Kings, probably out of print, but

41

easy to get still through a second-hand book-seller. There is also a little set of biographies by Mr. Meyer, a Baptist minister, not at all deep or scholarly, but interesting and full of illustrations, and really spiritual in tone. I do not want you to choke up your mind with other men's thoughts, or to express other men's thoughts instead of your own. But when you are young you feel at times that thoughts do not come too plentifully, and if you have read some good books and digested them and let the thoughts in them gradually affect your mental tissue, you will find a good deal of pleasure and advantage from working as I suggest.

In your second or third year you should be ready to face a series on the Apostles' Creed. Not necessarily consecutively; the subjects are too big for that at first. But have them ready to face on the first Monday that you are perplexed for a subject. You see what grand themes they give you—The Fatherhood of God; The Incarnation; The Passion; The Descent into Hades; The Resurrection, etc. Keep planning and collecting for these. The first week that you are at a loss for a subject turn to the drawer where you have been collecting material for a sermon on the Fatherhood of God, and go at it at once. Give a good week's work to it, and you will probably be delighted with the result; and, believe me, you will have learned a good deal of theology and given your people valuable teaching when you have read well for, and written carefully, that series of sermons.

Keep all these series of sermons carefully for further use. Certainly not to preach them again as they are. If you are really growing in your life you cannot do that. They will seem poor and crude to you in a few years, but if there is valuable thought in them use it. Destroy the old manuscript—write a new sermon, but the old one will have greatly helped you. The series of sermons on these subjects that I have suggested should be a valuable and permanent help all through your life, therefore, do your best at them.

I believe greatly in courses of sermons, if you can make short enough courses, and if you are sufficiently interested in them to make them very interesting to your people. I find that the people tire of a course if it exceeds about six sermons. But that depends on the preacher's power to interest them. Some of you might find it possible to keep up interest in much longer courses, and especially in a country

church where the people have not so many
other things to take up their attention. And in
this connection, let me say, our teaching would
become much more systematic if we had more
expository preaching. It is a great need. People do not learn the Bible, they do not learn
how full of interest a book of the Bible is when
rightly understood. I do not find it easy in a
town parish where the congregations change a
good deal, and where the same preacher does
not occupy exclusively the morning or evening
pulpit. But if I were the sole preacher in a
country church, I think, either at morning or
evening service, I should always have a book of
the Bible on hand. When I came to my present
parish I announced that I would try to teach
the main books of the Bible in ten years, giving
to it the first three months of each year. I
began with Genesis, it is an intensely interesting book. The Creation; the Fall; the story of
Abraham, Isaac, Jacob, and Joseph. The following year came the Life of Moses, then the
Prophets and Kings, the Life of Our Lord, the
Life and Letters of St. Paul, etc. So each year
for three months together I turned the whole
morning congregation into a huge Bible class,
and I was astonished and delighted at the pleas-

ure that these three months gave to myself and,
I think, to the people. They never seemed to
object to the length of the courses. I feel sure
many of you could do this; only if you try you
must beware of doing it minutely—just the
great broad lines of teaching and no more.[1]
A very good specimen of such work is F. W.
Robertson's Lectures on the Epistles to the
Corinthians.

§ 4

Now let us discuss some questions on which
opinion is divided. (1) Ought you to preach in
these early days about doubt and scepticism,
and discuss infidel theories in the pulpit? That
depends not only on what your congregation
is, but also, and chiefly, on what you are yourself. There are certain congregations that one
need never preach to on such subjects. But,
also, there are certain clergy who are not competent to deal effectively with such subjects.
Men who have never had any doubt or intellectual struggle, and who have no sympathy
with such. They may be very holy men, able to

[1] *Publisher's Note.*—The above lectures by the author are
now published in simple form in five small volumes, *The
Bible for School and Home* (George H. Doran Company).

help the main part of their congregation, perhaps better than most others could, but they
cannot understand or sympathise with, they
cannot put themselves in the place of the man
who is innately sceptical, to whom doubt comes
very much easier than belief. There are such
sceptical natures, good and faithful seekers
after God, and, therefore, surely acceptable to
God. I think if you have never had doubts or
difficulties yourself you will probably never be
as helpful to sceptics as the man who has
thought and doubted and agonised and fought
his way down to the solid bed-rock of faith for
himself. Not as helpful I say. But you can be
very helpful to the sceptic for all that, if the
real Christlike spirit of love is in you. For if
you, like your Master, are trying to make the
best, and think the best, and look for the best
in others, you will think the best of the man
who is honest in his doubt. You will believe it
quite possible for a doubter to be in earnest and
to be longing after God and righteousness.
For there is no sin in honest doubt. If a man
cannot believe what else can he do but doubt?
Get in sympathy with your doubter. Talk to
him. And thus you will be able to tell him that
doubt itself is not sin, and that the great

Father is looking with loving solicitude on His poor wandering children in the wood seeking the path home. Indeed if you feel thus I am not sure that your strong unquestioning faith will not be as great a help to the doubter as the sympathy which you would feel with him if you had been through the wood yourself. Make up your mind that there is a great deal of latent scepticism amongst men and amongst women too, in this age. But make up your mind, too, not to be over tender and over sentimental about it because a large part of it is very unreal —superficial objections picked up at second-hand and fostered through pure carelessness, or a desire to appear clever and thoughtful. There are the real earnest doubters, whose hearts are sore and who are longing for the light. But it is well to warn you that in my own experience, and it has been considerable, the majority who have doubts could get rid of them very easily if they were in real earnest. Therefore, in preaching about scepticism, while being very tender with one class, remind your audience that many belong to the other, and preach to such sternly and with reproof for the injury they are doing to the cause of God. This warning is necessary. I who had myself suf-

47

fered from doubts was, in the beginning of my
ministry, a great deal too tender and sentimental with a set of men who cared very little, and
who argued things with me largely for the intellectual interest.

(2) In this connection comes the question,
Should one preach about such subjects as Science and Religion? If you are competent to do
so, and if you have reason to believe that it
would be helpful in your parish, do so by all
means. If there are only a few who need it,
better do it in private conversation. But if you
can so present a scientific difficulty that men
may see it does not affect religion rightly understood, by all means preach it. But preach
such things seldom, and then preach them with
great care, writing the sermon and submitting
it to wise friends before preaching. For these
are very difficult things to say well within the
limits of a short sermon, and to say them badly
or incompletely will do far more harm than
good. On the whole, for your first five years,
when you will probably feel most prompted to
do it, you should be inclined to doubt your ca-
pacity for doing it well. If you try to do it at
all, be sure you do it with absolute honesty and
fairness. Be quite sure that you understand

your opponent. Assume that the opponents are
as honest men as yourself, and that they seriously believe what they say. Never attempt to
sneer, never attempt to rouse the *odium theo-
logicum,* never suggest that the effect of their
opinions on religious belief should prevent them
holding such opinions. It is nothing less than
insult to scientific men to ask that they should
be influenced in their search for truth by any
thought of the way in which their conclusions
would affect religious belief. Above all, never
understate, or unfairly state, their position. If
you touch controversy at all be absolutely generous and fair and honest. Do not try to lie
for God: do not try to cast out devils by Beel-
zebub, the prince of the devils.

About Higher Criticism, and questions of
inspiration of Scripture, I think you should
sometimes speak. If you believe that there is
nothing to be afraid of you should speak out
and say so. Don't imagine the people are not
thinking of it—they are. Especially should
you try gradually and steadily to correct those
old false views about the Bible and verbal inspiration, which are the chief stronghold of
sceptical attacks on Scripture. It is so easy for
sceptics to point out to simple people in the Old

49

Testament permitted usages that we would not tolerate to-day, and sentiments of inspired men, which, we feel, could not win the approval of Christ. Some time since a devout Christian lady, an earnest simple student of Scripture, came to me. A sceptical friend had been disturbing her belief in God and the Bible. He showed her how slavery was permitted in the inspired teaching, and plurality of wives, and that a man was allowed to divorce his wife for a slight reason. He pointed to the blessing on Jael and the Psalmist uttering prayers for vengeance on his foes. "And this," he sneered, "is the God of your devotion, this is your inspired Bible."

Much of the flippant popular scepticism comes from lack of teaching the people how to regard and how to read the Bible. Here, for example, my friend had to be taught of the progressive nature of God's revelation to the world—that the human race is as a gigantic man having to be taught gradually from childhood as he could bear it—that the old-world men were but in the lower classes of God's school—that the Old Testament was but preparatory to the higher teaching of Christ.

Teach the people how to read their Bible. It is a very important thing to do for them.

§ 5

With regard to "questions of the day" I think the preacher should deal with them at times when they are deeply occupying the thoughts of his people. It is his duty at such times to teach the relation of God's law to public duties and public questions, the use of the ballot, capital and labor disputes, etc. But not often. And only in order to bring religion as an "applied science" to bear on them. The only question for the preacher is, What would the Lord Jesus do? What would He say? And the preacher should be clear about the answer.

For example, in the burning question of Capital and Labor. I asked an educated working man one day, Why do not the workingmen come oftener to church? "Let the church come out boldly," he said, "as her Master would on the side of the masses, on the side of Labor against Capital. Then you would see the masses following Him as they did in Galilee." But that is not true. Her Master took no sides except that of Right against Wrong, of Un-

51

selfishness against Selfishness irrespective of classes. A partisan church would not represent Christ and would not in the long run attract even the workers. If Jesus did not flatter the rich neither did He flatter the poor. Of all who ever served the people He was the frankest. He held up His high ideals, Righteousness, Unselfishness, and left all to apply them to their individual cases. His church's business is to follow His lead. Here in the matter of production there are three partners, the Capitalist who provides means for labor; the Worker by hand or brain who produces or distributes; the Consumer without whom the others would have no place. Formerly the Capitalist usurped power over the others. Now the Worker is trying to do so. And the Consumer would probably do the same if he could. The Church's place is to represent her Lord, to say to Capitalist and Worker and Consumer alike, "Sirs, ye are brethren, why do ye wrong one to another? One is your Master even Christ and all ye are brethren."

But if the Church must not take sides in the warfare of classes who are now very well able to fight for themselves, there is one class that she must always take sides with, the poor, the helpless, the oppressed. And she has not been doing it. Often has their bitter cry gone up to her Lord, "Your Christians have been so busy saving their souls that they have no time to save us. There is great need in our day of emphasizing the duty of Social Service and especially in our cities. Such questions as the Housing of the Poor, Old Age Pensions, Playgrounds for children in the slums, etc., greatly need to be discussed with religious people. If ever the Church is to represent her Lord aright that the multitudes may follow Him she must go out into the open and champion the helpless. She must insist on the duty of Social Religion.

What do we mean by Social Religion? There are two favourite saints in the Greek Church, St. Cassian and St. Nicolaus. Cassian is the type of individual Christianity. He took great care of himself and his soul's salvation; he had six services a day with fasts and scourgings. Nicolaus was of another type. His life was spent in service. He helped the poor for Christ's sake. He tended the sick. He made little children happy. His name, St. Nicolaus, we have corrupted to Santa Claus.

Cassian, according to the legend, enters Heaven and is questioned by the Lord.

"What hast thou seen on earth, Cassian, as thou camest hither?"

"Lord, I saw a wagoner floundering in the mud."

"And didst thou help him?"

"Nay, Lord, I was coming into thy presence and I feared to soil my white robes."

Afterwards Nicolaus comes in all stained and soiled with mire.

"Why so stained and soiled, Nicolaus," asks the Lord.

"I saw a poor wagoner," said Nicolaus, "floundering in the mud and I had to put my shoulder to the wheel to help him out."

"Thou didst well, Nicolaus," said the Lord. "Thou, Cassian, since thou didst guard the white robes of thy baptism shall haul a day every year dedicated to thee. Thou, Nicolaus, since thou didst help thy brother out of the mud thou shalt have four."

Which things are an allegory. God will bless and prosper His church in proportion to the help which she gives to His poor children floundering in the mire for whom Christ died.

Which things are also an illustration of two types of religion in the church today. The first is occupied with the thought of one's own soul, one's own devotion to God, one's responsibility for one's own spiritual life. This we may call Individual Religion. Let no man make light of it in his enthusiasm for Social

Service. It has been in all ages the inspiration of saints and heroes who have placed above everything holiness of life. It is in the deepening of the Individual Religion lies the hope for the future of the Church and of the world. But as it deepens and strengthens it will remain no more Individual Religion. As religion grows there comes to it its crown and blossom. More of the Christlikeness passes into it, the love and pity for all our fellowmen, the pain at all the evils which beset them, the indignation against all the wrong that is done them, the generous enthusiasm to spend and be spent for them, the resolve that they shall get the chance at least to live out the best that is in them.

If your "topical sermons" deal with subjects of this kind you may safely regard them as "preaching Christ." But for the general topics of the day be chary of dealing with them. People in church do not want the pabulum of the newspapers. There is a need in their hearts more often than you know, "Sir, we would see Jesus."

LECTURE III

PLACERE

Lecture III

PLACERE

§ 1

I want here to emphasise a matter of vital necessity in your preaching which usually is by no means emphasised as it should be. I mean the habit of interesting your people, holding their attention right through your sermon. I call it a habit rather than a power because I think it is possible for any intelligent man to do it if he will take the trouble and acquire the habit.

Do you know Cicero's essentials of oratory:

1. *Placere* (to interest).
2. *Docere* (to teach).
3. *Movere* (to move).

The second and third of course go without saying. Unfortunately what that wise old Roman placed as the first seems regarded by many preachers as of minor importance. Of course

it is not much good to do the *Placere* if you do
not go on from it to the *Docere* and *Movere*.
But still the *Placere* is what wants the especial
emphasis, since it seems so commonly ignored.
Whole hosts of preachers who have a good deal
to teach people and who are eager to move people, seem to go on year after year without any
sore searchings of heart as to whether they are
"interesting" these people. I do not see much
good in your valuable teaching and in your
vehement exhorting, if the people are surrep-
titiously glancing at their watches to see if the
twenty minutes is nearly up.

§ 2

There are two axioms which I desire to lay
down—(1) Preaching is of no use at all unless
you can make the people listen to it; (2) It is
possible for us all, more or less, to make them
listen.

I think it was Archbishop Magee that described in a sentence the three types of preachers. "There are some preachers," he said,
"whom you *cannot* listen to; there are some
preachers whom you *can* listen to; there are
some preachers whom you *must* listen to." I

think there is a considerable number of the first, a very great number of the second, and extremely few of the third—extremely few—and I do not believe this need be so. In fact I am quite sure it need not, and, therefore, I want you to increase the ranks of the third, and to make up your minds that if work and study and anxiety about it will do anything, you are determined in your future ministry to make men listen to you.

And with that in view, I want you first not to excuse yourselves by the common cant of the so-called "religious world" about the distaste that people have for hearing about religion. Don't you believe it. It is a great comfort to a dull, stupid preacher who has not put any enthusiasm into his sermon, or taken any thought or trouble to make it interesting to the people, to console himself for the bored, uninterested look of his audience by the reflection that the fault is not in his sermon but in the distaste of "the natural man" for religious teaching. It would be amusing if it were not so sad to hear him say with calm self-satisfaction that his business is to preach God's Word whether men hear or forbear. Ah! if he could but hear the opinions of his audience, not only of the careless but of those also who are caring to be helped; if he could mingle with the people coming out of church and hear the very unflattering comments as to the length and diffuseness and platitudes of his sermon, it might be a very salutary experience. We clergy do not hear half enough of what the laity say of us. It would be better if we did. This poor patient laity! I think they deserve great sympathy. It is perfectly exasperating the way that intelligent lay people are treated by lazy and self-sufficient preachers. One does not wonder that many of them have been driven off from church. Recently I was away in Switzerland at a favourite English resort, and had many serious talks with lay people from various places, and the two things that most impressed me were the complaints that we clergy preach such uninteresting sermons, and the revelation that a great many seemingly careless people are really wanting to learn and to be interested.

Now you must take men as they are. The general congregation may not be very eager to hear what you have got to say, but they are, as a rule, quite willing to listen to you. Indeed as they have to sit still during the sermon, in any case, the most careless of them would rather listen and be interested than not; and if they are interested and listen, you may be sure that after the sermon is over a good deal of thought will be given to what you have said, and if you have got into the habit of interesting them, they will get into the habit of listening, and into the habit of thinking too, about what you have said to them. I should like you to give this thought full entrance into your minds, that your people are willing enough to listen if you make it worth while for them; and that, therefore, if your congregation seem habitually dull and uninterested you should, at least, have grave searchings of heart as to whether the fault is not in yourself. Some stupid person may object, that this is making too much of our own human efforts, and tell us that GOD can use very dull sermons to the helping of men's souls. Of course that is so, and it is very well that it is, for there are certainly plenty of dull sermons to be so used. But surely such talk is utter rubbish. Surely (other things being equal) it is likely that God will use for most good the sermon that has been best listened to by the people.

§ 3

First, then, drive the conviction deep into your mind that you CAN make people listen if you are willing to pay the price. I know a good many uninteresting preachers. Some have not yet discovered that they are uninteresting. They are beyond hope. Some have discovered it and rest there believing that they lack the gift and cannot help it. There is some hope for them.

You CAN make people listen. Some, of course, can do it more than others. Some men have a personal magnetism which commands attention. But we can all be really interesting preachers if we want to, and therefore it is sin and shame to fail in being so. In the next chapter I deal with the most serious cause of this failure. Here I just offer a few obvious suggestions.

(1) Have something to say. And say it in as few words as you can. And then stop. I once heard a chairman put it to the speakers at a meeting, "Stand up. Speak up. Shut up."

Stand up in your pulpit not because you have *to say something* but because you have *some-*

thing to say. Make sure of that first. Then say it. Don't preach it or elaborate it. Just say it as simply and naturally as you would say it in conversation. And say it in the fewest words that you can. Cut out of your sermon every word that can be dispensed with. Put yourself in the position of a speaker at an impatient public meeting with the dread of the chairman's bell waiting to ring you down— where you must say your best and say it effectively before you are "caught out." This does not mean that you must always preach a short sermon, but that you must preach it in the shortest time possible to you. The pulpit to-day is complaining of the impatient demand for short sermons. It serves the pulpit right. It is the Nemesis of much windy talking in the past. This impatience has harm in it. We are getting fewer of the great sermons on great subjects which cannot be briefly handled. But there is some gain in it too. The sermon becomes stronger by condensation. And great subjects will still be listened to at some length if they are treated effectively without superfluous words. I have heard capital sermons of less than fifteen minutes and I have heard preachers not distinguished strangers but clergy of the parish listened to without impatience for nearly an hour. But the rule held for the long sermon as the short, that the points were effectively put, and in as few words as the subject permitted. Cut out every sentence that is not accomplishing something, which will usually mean a good many sentences. And when you have said what you want, stop. And stop effectively. Don't run around like a dog after his tail. Prepare your ending.

(2) When your sermon is prepared go over it carefully with the question, Is it interesting? Are there dull pages in it? Could I enliven them by illustrations or otherwise? Keep on the lookout for telling illustrations from your reading. But they should be few and brief and clear and to the point. An illustration that does not illustrate is only a distraction.

(3) Seek to have variety in your sermons and in your treatment of subjects. Some preachers have a dead uniformity of treatment however different the subject and their sermons stand like a dull uniform row of workmen's cottages in a street. Seek variety of treatment. For example, if one sermon about missions is a solid statement of the Church's duty and the condition of heathendom let your next be the

romantic, exciting life of a famous missionary and the lessons which it brings. If you are arguing the pros and cons of a certain subject put it sometimes in form of a dialogue. Find striking beginnings for sermons or for each section of a sermon. Try to surprise people. Do everything you can to sustain interest and keep attention from flagging so long as you do nothing unworthy the solemnity of your subject.

(4) Ask yourself in every sermon, Could the man in the pew tell his wife—or rather in these days, Could the woman in the pew tell her husband in two sentences the central thought of your sermon? If not, why not?

(5) I think, too, it is a good thing to study attractive speeches and sermons, not for their thoughts, but to see how the speaker arranged his subject, how he began and ended, how he led up to his striking points, what devices he used to sustain attention, in a word, to find out what made his discourse interesting.

These are but a few obvious suggestions. In the next chapter I speak of the power of "Grip" which will count more than aught else in making your people listen.

§ 4

Now we come to the question, what can you do to make the people listen? Mind, you *can* make them listen if you are willing to pay the price. Of course, some can do it more than others. Some men have a personal magnetism, a personal enthusiasm, which commands the attention. But even to some of us who have no such advantages, this power of grip may belong. We, too, may interest people if we are willing to work, and it is a sin and a shame for us to fail in doing it, especially if we have plenty of time for preparation. The secret is simple enough. Your sermon will grow more interesting to the people and more effective in influencing the intellect and conscience in proportion as you have—

(1) MORE LABOUR IN THINKING OUT,

(2) MORE COURAGE IN SPEAKING OUT, the full revelation that God has committed to you. It is for want of these that our sermons lack interest, and become vague and hazy and lose grip of the people. Let me speak of these two things separately.

68

LECTURE IV

THE QUALITY OF "GRIP"

Lecture IV

THE QUALITY OF "GRIP"

§ 1

Archbishop Sancroft once asked Betterton the tragedian, "How is it that when you speak everybody listens to you although you speak fiction, but when we speak the people do not listen though we speak the words of Divine truth?"

"I think, your Grace," replied the actor, "the reason is this, you speak truth as though you believed it to be fiction, whilst we speak fiction as though we believed it to be truth."

We have to acknowledge that there are grounds for this criticism. What is the cause? Not insincerity or doubt about the facts which we teach but chiefly failure to realise them, to grip them as realities, often deep, fascinating, exciting realities. Many a preacher is a mere juggler with phrases, floating on a sea of *words,* not getting down to *things.* So the preacher loses power in preaching. So the people lose interest in listening.

I speak to you now of this quality of "Grip," the habit of clear, sharp gripping the ideas which lie behind the words and phrases that we use. I am thinking here mainly of *intellectual* grip of *ideas*. But I must not pass over the *imaginative* grip, if I may so call it, the power of "putting yourself in his place"—of seeing the scenes and entering into the feelings about which you are writing or preaching.

Why does a mother read with flushed and tearful face the tale of a woman's self-sacrifice for her child? Why is there such intense interest for a schoolboy in a graphic story of adventure? Because unconsciously, without effort, the imagination is going forth, living in the scene, experiencing every feeling of the actors, obeying that law which is the great secret of pleasurable reading—*put yourself in his place*. Now if one take pains to acquire the habit it is always possible to do this in some degree at least; not always indeed unconsciously and without effort—sometimes it requires a good deal of effort, especially in books so familiar to us as are those of the Bible. But it is worth all the effort it costs. The amount of

72

interest in any part will depend greatly on our success in thinking ourselves into the place of the persons concerned, not merely in picturing the outward scene, but also, in so far as may be, entering into the minds of the speakers and actors. True, a greater imaginative power will give one man an advantage over another, but all that is really needful for success is some little knowledge of the circumstances and surroundings, and the effort to think oneself thoroughly into them.

Of course this is easier in some parts than in others. It is easy, for instance, to make the lump rise in one's throat when thinking how Jacob and Joseph met at Tel-el-Kebir. It is easy in reading about Elijah, to put yourself in his place in his indignant wrath against Ahab at Naboth's field, or in his mocking exultation over the prophets of Baal. It is easy to feel the pathos of Moses' farewell, to put yourself in the place of Deborah in the joy of her triumph, or of the big, mischievous giant with the gates of Gaza on his back, laughing at the surprise of the outwitted Philistines. The historical books of the Old and New Testament are full of such scenes, and any man who will exercise his imaginative faculty has material for the most vivid pictures. But what I desire to emphasise is, that not only here, but all through the Bible it is possible to add a keen interest to your reading by this effort to "put yourself in his place." Think, for instance, in the early prophecies of Isaiah of a vacillating king and an evil-living people, of the rumours in the city of approaching invasion, and the solemn sight of the prophet in his haircloth robe proclaiming the Divine message that burned within him. In the Gospels try to enter into the feelings of the formalist Pharisees and the jealous scribes and the ignorant people from the slums of Jerusalem, and above all of the great loving, sympathising heart of Him Who understood them all. Try as you preach the epistles of St. Paul to put yourself in the place of the writer, with his sensitive, highly-strung nature, now glad, now despondent, now vexed and dissatisfied at the conduct of some church, but always with every thought full of loving loyalty to his Master.

§ 2

But I have said I am thinking mainly of the intellectual grip, the clear, sharp *gripping of the ideas* which lie behind the words and

74

phrases that we use. It is the great defect of us theologians—we do not think out vigorously and clearly, and the consequence is a vagueness and haziness and a cultivating of platitudes, which takes all the interest and grip out of our sermons. Do you remember Mephistopheles' advice to Faust in the play, "Busy yourself with *words*. Do not trouble yourself about *things.*" Yes, that is it. Do not trouble yourself about *things*. That has been the devil's advice to theologians since theology began. There are tremendously and magnificently grand things behind the words and phrases which we use, things full of awe and mystery and absorbing interest. But we do not get hold of them. We pay ourselves off with words, as with counters in a game. So we feel vague and hazy, we clergy, and our sermons become vague and hazy and fail to take hold. I used to think in my early ministry that it was only the young clergy that felt thus vague and hazy, until I began to attend clerical meetings and to ask definite questions, when I found, to my surprise, and perhaps to my comfort, that the minds of some of my elder brethren were not so pellucidly clear either on the great questions that they taught. We have not sufficiently acquired the habit of gripping firmly and seeing clearly the great ideas which lie behind the religious words and phrases which we use. It is only by degrees this dawns on some of us. I honestly think that we have no conception of the interest and enthusiasm and wonder, that we should get in our religious teaching if we only got to the reality of it; that we have no conception of the loss to Christian men and women through careless thinking, through haziness and woolliness of mind, through not trying to grip firmly and see clearly the great ideas that lie behind the words and phrases which we use in the pulpit.

§ 3

You see what I mean? Take, for example, "the Gospel." If I ask any Sunday-school child the meaning of the word, he will say, *good news,* something to *make people glad.* Now does it always convey that meaning? I doubt it very gravely. If a man who had never heard of Christianity were to learn the Gospel first from the preaching in some of our churches, I fear he would not be much impressed with the goodness or gladness of it. The word has got so dulled and rounded by much use that the sharp edges have got rubbed off it. It has become so hackneyed and covered over with commonplace and platitude, that the idea of good news, glad, joyous, inspiriting news, does not usually strike one at all, and people listen to Gospels that are by no means good news or glad news, Gospels utterly incapable of stirring their pulses and gladdening their hearts. I think if you dropped the word "Gospel" for a while and used only the word "good news" you might sharpen up and put interest into the word, and keep yourselves from believing some very stupid things that are called Gospel to-day.

I remember a description of the Christian Gospel by a non-Christian writer, sneering at Christianity. He pictures a missionary teaching a poor Chinaman. "The Gospel means, first of all, you are a sinner and radically corrupt and evil, and therefore justly exposed to the wrath of God and everlasting punishment. That is the first part of the Christian Gospel." "Well now," says the poor Chinaman, "if the Gospel means good news, I don't think that is good news. It is news, certainly, but I don't think it is good news." "But," says the preacher, "the Gospel is more than that. God offers you forgiveness and happiness. If you believe in the Atonement and in certain other doctrines, and love God, and repent of your sins, God will take you to Heaven. If not, He will put you into everlasting torment, where you will live in infinite agony and infinite sin for ever and ever and ever." "I don't think," replies the poor Chinaman, "that that is at all good news, for, perhaps, I cannot believe these things, or love this God who is going, perhaps, to do these terrible things to me. That Gospel of yours is news, certainly, but it does not seem to me to be very good news."

As I read this parody of the Gospel I could not help feeling that it is not so very much exaggerated. The popular notion of the Gospel amongst our lay people is often rather like that. Fancy any one calling that good news! or thinking that was the glad tidings of great joy which made the angels burst through Heaven at Christmastide. Surely, if people would grip the idea of glad news the absurdity of such Gospels would strike them at once, and they would try to find out what men had to be so glad about.

The "Gospel," rightly understood, is full of grip, full of the power of rousing enthusiasm and awe and mystery and deep absorbing interest. I say it, unhesitatingly looking common-sense men in the face, that no speakers have such rousing subjects as we have, that no study has a tithe of the interest that is in the full, fearless presentation of the whole Gospel of Christ. When you grip the ideas that lie behind the words, then only you get a full Gospel. But that full Gospel, throbbing with mystery and awe, and interest and joyous enthusiasm, requires thinking and studying, and a determination to get at realities, and a big fearless faith in God. It does not lie on the surface for conventional makers of platitudes to find it. You must think, and muse, and meditate, and be alone with God, and let your mind and your soul and your heart play over the teaching till it glows and becomes alive and grips hold of you.

§ 4

Take another example. A preacher is preaching on the text, "God is love." It does not rouse him in the least, it has become so hackneyed, so covered over with commonplace platitudes, that it has no power over him. It has become too rounded; it does not grip him, and does not grip his people. But some day, like an inspiration, it catches him, and he never more can preach platitudes about it again.

His little sick boy is on his knee, and he fears the little lad may die. Is there anything, he thinks, that I would not do to save that little boy? Is there anything I would not do for his good, if he recovers? In this life I would work night and day for him. In "that" life I would go into the outer darkness for ever for him, if it would save my little lad from going there. If he went wrong my love for him would make me punish him, ay, perhaps punish him terribly—but if love and punishment failed I think my heart would break. "O God," he thinks, "how life here and hereafter would be one endless pain, how Heaven would be absolutely useless to me if that little boy were lost at the last."

Slowly and fully he lets that thought grip him, and then he wonderingly repeats to himself the little Creed that Christ has taught, "If ye then being evil know how to care thus for your children, how much more does the Heavenly Father." And in a moment the revelation has flashed on him. He asks himself: "Is that the meaning of the love of God; does it mean a vivid, real, palpitating thing like my love for my boy? Does it mean that He feels and cares and suffers for the little chap as I do —ay, that He must suffer for ever if He lose that boy? If I, being evil, must suffer, how much more must God? Is the pain in my heart, which would make me go to hell itself to save my child, but a faint reflection of the eternal pain in the heart of the Good Shepherd which sends him out for ever on the desolate mountains seeking that which is lost until He find it?" Perhaps he may not believe in such love of God, but, at any rate, he sees the meaning of it. It has gripped him. He knows the meaning now. "If it does not mean the feelings that I have in my heart when I am thinking of my little boy's future I do not know what it means. But oh! if it does mean that—that God actually does care and suffer, and by the necessity of His nature must for ever care and suffer like that—then nothing in the whole world matters in comparison with it. It is good to be alive in spite of all our troubles, good for me, good for my boy, good for every poor child of man; however awful may be the penalty of his wrong-doing, God cares! By the necessity of His nature He must for ever care!

"God's in His Heaven,
 All's right with the world."

Ah! he knows the meaning now. His face is flushing, his eyes are brightening with it. That man will preach no more dull platitudes about the love of God. His sermon on the love of God will grip next time.

§ 5

(1) Another example. I suppose if I were to put the question now to you all, what is the first and chiefest subject that you must preach? you would reply, "Christ; we must preach Christ." Surely yes. And yet—and yet—surely there must be right and wrong ways of preaching Christ; a way that will grip men, and a way that will leave them listless. Whilst writing this lecture I asked a thoughtful lay friend, whose opinion about sermons I greatly value, What would you expect if you were told of a certain preacher's subject next Sunday that he was going to preach Christ? "I should expect a rather stupid sermon," was the prompt reply. And, I fear, there was in my friend's experience some reason for the reply. I fear I have heard a good many men preaching

82

Christ, without being very much interested by them. But on the day of that reply I had been reading a story of the days of Gustavus Adolphus, of Sweden. The writer had not concealed his faults, but he made me admire and love him in spite of them. He made me feel angry with the nobles who thwarted him, and almost lonely for the moment as I read of the poor king's death. The writer did not make any demand for my love or admiration of the king. He just simply presented him to me as he appeared to his own enthusiasm—and thus he won me to him. I think something like that must be the meaning of preaching Christ. I wish I were capable of preaching Him thus. Some men are. I want you to be. I want you, at any rate, to see that to preach about His life and His Atonement platitudes that rouse no enthusiasm, and sentiments that you do not feel deeply yourself, is not preaching Christ, that to tell people they ought to love, and be touched by this love and self-sacrifice, is but whipping up their feelings as you would whip up a dead horse. You must just present Christ, and leave your picture to rouse enthusiasm. But you cannot do that without feeling enthusiasm yourself. You cannot grip your hearers unless

Christ has gripped you. The personal Christ must be real to you. You must have thought and meditated on Him till He has grown to be very real to you. You must study Him and think of Him till you can make men feel that He is as near, and as much alive, as when men of old heard His voice and looked into His eyes. That He is still the very Christ who took that little boy on His knee long ago, and grew stern and indignant at the thought of one tempting that child—the very Christ who made excuses for His sleeping disciples at Gethsemane, and looked for the good in every one around Him; who even saw, as He looked at the howling mob on Calvary, that some of them would be sorry by and by, and remembered that they were half mad with excitement—remembered, doubtless, that many of them had often been kind to their friends and little children. "They are mad with excitement," He thought; "Father, forgive them, for they do not know just now what they are doing."

Try to make His character real to yourself, as my author did with that poor, faulty Swedish king. For some of us it will take years to do it, but we cannot otherwise preach Christ, so that the subject will grip, so that people will long to come to Him.

§ 6

Take another subject. Any man who reads up theological books about it can preach about the Holy Communion, and the people can listen quietly and go home, and the altar-rails can remain deserted as before. But wait till some day when the subject has gripped him—gripped him. He has had to stop talking conventionally—he has had to go down to the reality beneath the words. It is easy to preach cold, correct theology about "the Body and Blood of Christ, which are verily and indeed taken and received," etc. But when a man refuses to play any longer with words, as if they were counters, and wants to get down to the realities underneath the words. When he demands of himself, "What is the thing which these words imply? What do I mean? Is it something real? Is there in any real sense a communicating of the nature of Christ Himself to a man in that Sacrament? Is there, next Sunday morning, going to take place in my simple little church a stupendous miracle? Will the living Christ be actually present, invisible as when

85

He stood by the Magdalen in the Easter dawn, as when He stood unseen with the disciples in the upper-room? Is this thrilling thing true or is it not true?" Is it true that in that sacrament the life of Christ passes into the life of men as when in transfusion of blood the lifeblood of a virile man passes into the veins of an anæmic patient? I do not just now want to advocate High views or Low views about the Sacraments. I want now only to plead for deep views—deep, reaching down and gripping for some reality underneath the words. But I think that never more will the Holy Communion be an uninteresting thing in that man's preaching. Never more will the Holy Table be deserted in that Church.

§ 7

There are hosts of other subjects.

Have you cleared your mind about conscience and its authority, and the startling fact that all over the world to-day from the Mississippi to the Ganges, from the Arctic to the Equator, no man is found without the sense of right and wrong, without the Divine imperative of the "ought" and "ought not" which stamps him indelibly as belonging to God.

Have you cleared your mind about its relation to Scripture, and what men are to do if conscience and Scripture seem to come into collision with each other? The man in the pew has been thinking a good deal about that, when he has had to take his part in the Imprecatory Psalms. In fact, the man in the pew has been thinking about a good many other things of late since the War time, and especially in the city parishes he is expecting that his clergy should have some clearer acquaintance with the relations of dogmatic theology to the religious questions that are in the air. He is greatly interested just now about death and the hereafter. They used to be dull and uninteresting subjects in our preaching. Not so now. The man in the pew wants to know if the moment of death fixes a man's destiny and stereotypes his state for all eternity. The woman in the pew wants to know if you think her careless boy, who was killed by a German bullet, is damned, or if there is such a thing as hope after death. She wants to know how any woman could enjoy a happy heaven while any human being belonging to her is in hell. Oh, the torture and eagerness I have seen in people who have been asking me these questions. It is not my province here to answer such questions for you. But it certainly is my province to insist that you must not play with words here. You must go to the realities, and try to find some answer, to form some opinion for yourself. Your power of grip in your preaching about it depends on this.

Have you ever realised the enthralling interest than can attach to a sermon on the Intermediate Life? The life of the waiting soul before the Judgment. The Bible teaches us that no man has ever yet gone to heaven; no man has ever yet gone to hell. All who ever lived on earth are waiting, still, waiting the coming of the day of God. Have you thought much about that waiting life which is so much in men's thoughts now! Have you realised what a great deal can be learned about it? How could any man think of such things without wonder and excitement! Is there any novel ever written, so full of wondrous interest as the thought of that world full of the great saints and heroes, and the dear ones who are neither saints nor heroes, that have lately gone away from us. There are men for whom a

88

great sorrow has forced open the doors of that unseen land, and they have been holding them open ever since for their people. They have been reading, and studying, and thinking, and in some little degree teaching wherever they could find any firm Scriptural foothold to go upon. That there is no death. That Death means but birth into a larger life. That as the baby's eyes open from the darkness of the womb to sunlight in this world so do the eyes that have closed in the darkness of death open on "a light that never was on sea or land." And it has revolutionised life for them. And it has opened the hearts of poor bereaved ones in their parishes who had no one to talk to them about the life in the unseen. The fact is, it has gripped them, and will not let them go, and when they preach on that particular subject which has gripped them so strongly, they can certainly grip the people. They can make them listen.

So men preach dull sermons, or weak sermons, or irritating sermons about the Church because they have not realised to themselves that great central enthusiasm of Christ about His "Kingdom of God" on earth. His very first sermon was about it; His very last words

before the Ascension were about it. All his
parables were illustrations of it. It seemed to
fill up His outlook into the future. No man
can realise that without growing deeply interested, without feeling how impossible it is to
fully preach Christ without preaching the
Church.

Such illustrations might go on indefinitely,
but time forbids. Surely I have said enough to
show you the vital importance of gripping down
deep for the realities that underlie the words
and phrases which you are using. Get the
habit of doing this. And get the habit while
you are young. When you are twenty years in
orders it will be almost impossible to begin.
When you have become Canons and Deans and
Archdeacons you will be "past praying for."

§ 8

The first requisite in thus gripping the realities is *more labour in thinking out* the truths
which God has revealed to us. And here let
me add a further requisite, *more courage in
speaking out* these truths when we have found
them. For this is important for the deepening

of your own grip as well as for its value in the instruction of your people.

The lack of this courage in speaking out is responsible for a good deal of uninteresting preaching. Yet I would rather you learned this a little later on. The picture flashes on me of the bumptious young preacher who thinks a little, or thinks that he thinks, and insists on being courageous and original and a superior fellow altogether, and so becomes a nuisance, with his crude, undigested theories. I beseech you again, be very humble and modest and reverent in seeking God's truth. "I beseech you," said Cromwell to some of his Ironside preachers, "I beseech you by the tender mercies of God, to believe that you may sometimes be mistaken." For your first five years do not try to be "courageous" or "original." You have two eyes and two ears and only one tongue. Read a great deal, listen to your elders a great deal, speak little. But when you are older, when you have made certain of a truth, when you know that all Bible students worthy the name are with you, when you hear that truth acknowledged at clerical meetings as an esoteric truth, that it would not be safe to teach people at present, then if you believe that that truth

will help the struggling and comfort the bereaved and solemnise the communicant, ask
God's help that you may not—

> "in silence shrink
> From the truth you needs must think."

And a rich reward will come to you in the
delight of your preaching and in the gratitude
of your best people.

But you will have many temptations to hold
your tongue. You will find that some of your
people do not want to be made think. You will
have some of them calling you High Church,
or Broad Church, if you put thoughts before
them that they have not been accustomed to,
e.g., if you present realities, not mere words,
about the Sacraments, the Church, the Future
Life, the love and the pain of God for men.
And perhaps some people will whisper that you
are not quite a "safe man," which is a very terrible accusation in some parts of the Church.
We have a great deal too much of this "safe-
ness" in our day; I heartily wish we had less
of it; it is a great source of weakness to the
Church, and our most thoughtful laymen are
getting sick of it already. There is a certain
sort of "safe man," who will always be hon-

oured—the wise, calm, thoughtful pastor, who thinks deeply and speaks fearlessly, but speaks always tactfully and avoids obnoxious phrases in his teaching of deep truths. But alas, the "safe man" too commonly means the man who does not think, and does not make anybody else think, who has never stood on the unpopular side, and never taught an unpopular doctrine. We have a great deal too many such. God keep you young men from that contemptible ambition of being a "safe man," clipping and trimming the full Gospel of Christ. You are not being ordained for that; you are not being commissioned for that. You are to be sent out from this place as Christ's ambassadors, to preach to men, at any cost, "the whole counsel of God."

LECTURE V

PREPARING THE SERMON

Lecture V

PREPARING THE SERMON

Our subject to-day is the "Preparation of the Sermon"—I mean the special preparation of the special sermon to be preached on the following Sunday. In a sense—and a very real sense—all that I have said to you up to this has been "on the preparation of the sermon." I have tried to show you that the first process, the foundation of all sermon preparation, is the preparation of the preacher himself, the making and training and disciplining of a man fit to be a vehicle of God's Truth to his fellows. That will be for you the work of a lifetime; and God will do a great deal of it for you apart from your intention altogether. To me it is touching to look in your faces to-day; to think of the true hearts amongst you of whom God will make His faithful preachers in the future; to think of all that God's life preparation must mean to you, of steady, patient struggle after communion with God, of prayer and penitence,

97

of bitter dissatisfaction with yourself and your efforts: perhaps of keen, agonising discipline, of sorrow to get you into full sympathy with the people you are to help; but also of the gladness and hopefulness, of the joy of success in helping men, of eager aspirations, of flashes of enthusiasm for right, and of joyful insight into the boundless, unutterable love of God— all the strange, tender, thrilling experiences which, to every true heart amongst you, will be God's "preparation for the sermon." Yes, that is the great life-long preparation.

And then, too, I have tried to show you that the *study* in the preparation of each sermon is also lifelong. All the wide reading of a lifetime will influence, in some degree, every sermon. All your study of Scripture, of theology, of travel, of science; even the thoughts that have been roused in you by the fiction that you have read to rest your mind. Every Sunday sermon will be the better or the worse for the reading or the neglect of reading in your previous life. I beseech you, read, *read,* READ. Hear Dr. Arnold: "I must read. I will not give my boys to drink out of stagnant water." Many do this. So, you see, the preparation for the sermon and the study for the sermon **are** lifelong.

§ 1

But now I am thinking of the special sermon to be preached on the next Sunday. And the first thought that comes to me is, "When are you going to prepare it?" I am assuming all through these lectures that I have to deal with serious, earnest men. I assume that I have no need of telling you not to let your sermon lie over to the end of the week, and then rush on Saturday to commentaries and books of sermons to get together a crude, undigested discourse which will get you somehow over the Sunday. No serious man who realises the meaning of preaching needs to be warned against that.

Your sermon must be running through your mind during the whole week, however busy otherwise you may be. You may tell me that this is but a counsel of perfection; that in the present rush of parish work that cannot be done. I do not believe it. There is too much fussy talk of this kind amongst clergy. There is no rush of parish work anywhere such as would prevent the due preparation of your

99

sermon and it will be only your own indolence and want of system that will make you imagine that there is. If you are willing to do your work as systematically and punctually as the business men in your parish, there will be no difficulty. But if you get up at half-past eight, and breakfast at half-past nine, and read the paper and idle about till half-past ten, and have petty parish interruptions till half-past eleven, you have no right to talk about the pressure of duties and the want of time for sermon preparation. I have warned you before of this habit. It is the ruin of half the young clergy. To the man who indulges in it and spoils his sermons I can only say, and very sternly, that he is sinning deliberately against God, and some day, when his eyes are opened, will bitterly repent of it. I do not think any other set of men waste their time as much as we clergy do, nor talk as much about the many interruptions and the many engagements that prevent their being hard students. Whenever I hear a man, at any rate outside the busy centres, talk like that, I feel pretty sure that that man is wasting his time, and has no fixed, punctual, systematic habits of work. You have no right to work less hours in the day than a hard-

worked business man works. You have no
right to be less punctual and systematic in your
work.

Settle it with yourselves that the supreme
work of the week is the Sunday sermon, or
sermons. I do not want you to make light of
visiting, or classes, or all the other engagements. You should have plenty of time for
them all if you are systematic. If not let some
of them go. But you must see for yourself that
no other such opportunity can come to you as
that Sunday hour when a large number of
people of all sorts come together and will sit
still and listen for twenty minutes to the very
best you can give them. Fancy any man wasting his time during the week and then daring
to stand up in the presence of God and of that
congregation to preach a poor, unhelpful, uninteresting sermon!

I feel very sternly about this, for it is my
own temptation. So I repeat to you again, you
must work; you must plod systematically at
your sermons, with the grain and against the
grain, in the mood and out of the mood. I
used to imagine in my younger days that I
could do no good at my sermon when I was
out of the mood for it. And, no doubt, it was

true that I could sometimes, when eager and excited about my subject, do more and better work in an hour than I could at another time in half a week. But I learned by experience that my indolent mind, if allowed to have its own way, would very often be out of the mood. I believe even our novelists and writers of books in which mood means a great deal, have come to the same conclusion and found that a man, to do real good work in his study, must go to it and plod at it as steadily as the man breaking stones on the road.

How much time should you give to study and preparation for your sermon? Three hours a day, if you are in a busy parish, not necessarily all at once. In the country considerably more. I think the people in the quiet country parishes ought to be in the most enviable position in the whole Church. They should get the most interesting and thoughtful and well-prepared sermons. A man in a quiet village who is willing to give nine hours a day to his work, could easily give five to the Sunday sermons. I know quite well all that is against him—the depression, the small numbers, the want of that quick friction of mind with mind which keeps the town man at pleasant high pressure and makes speaking and writing easier to him. But, all the same, I say to you whose lot will lie in the country village, you ought to preach the best sermons of us all.

Whatever time you can give, let it be at the best hours of the day. If the morning is your best time, do not fritter it away by answering your morning letters. They can be done at other times. If there are too many other things to do—drop some of these other things. I think some of our parishes would be the better of a little less fussing on week days, and a little more thought and work at the sermon for Sunday. If too important to drop, then rearrange them.

Emphatically I say to you, Get up early, get your best hours unbroken at your sermon; go at it punctually, go at it daily. Avoid interruptions. I have somewhere met the advice that, if necessary, you should get a wife, or a cross housekeeper, or a big dog, or something to keep interruptions from you. In my last parish I put a notice in the Parish Magazine asking that no one should call on me without special reason between nine and twelve o'clock, and it had a very good effect.

§ 2

Happy for you if you have only one weekly sermon to prepare, so that you can put your best into it. If you must prepare two put your best into one of them, and for the other preach an old sermon rewritten, or keep an easy series, such as the parables, for extempore teaching, or far better, keep a book of the Bible, to be carefully studied at the evening service in the way that I have already suggested. Very few men can prepare two good sermons in a week, and it is a waste of power to prepare two poor sermons. A course of expository teaching is much easier to prepare than a second sermon, and probably much better for the people.

I have already told you the importance of preaching regularly on the subjects of the Christian year. I have told you what I thought of the value of courses of sermons and of expository teaching, and not the least of the advantages is that they will help to set you free from worrying over a subject for Sunday. You must do everything you can to keep yourself from that worry. I recommend to you Canon Liddon's habit of reading every night a good printed sermon. That would suggest many valuable thoughts and very frequently suggest splendid subjects for sermons. I recommend you to have a Bible interleaved with blank pages on which you can note sermons or articles bearing on certain texts. These should help your sermon. Only the sermon must be your own sermon though suggested by another. It must be your thoughts passed through your personality. I think it is quite allowable especially in your younger days that you should take hold of a really valuable sermon that has interested you and get hold of its leading thoughts and write a sermon with it as a basis. When a thought is a very striking one acknowledge the source of it. But generally speaking published thoughts that have really gripped you have thus become your own and may be freely used. Only, for you own soul's sake guard against literary dishonesty. The sermon must express your thought and feeling. It must be *your* sermon. To avoid all mistakes let me say here once for all, that the man who takes another man's sermon into the pulpit and delivers it as his own is a liar, and dishonest, and utterly unfit for the sacred office of the ministry.

I recommend you in all your reading to keep a book of "loose leaf" sheets beside you to jot down your thoughts and suggestions for sermons. As you read your daily Bible portion, with a good commentary; as you read the sermons of the famous sermon writers; as you read the Church papers, the daily newspaper, the novel, in your idle hour, anything and everything you read, thoughts and suggestions will come to you which should be jotted down at once. Sometimes the whole idea of a sermon will come to you. Sometimes separate thoughts or illustrations—jot them down as fully as you can, with a title across the top. Keep them in a drawer; go over them regularly. Sometimes several of them will go together and form a basis for a sermon. More often you will take up one suggested by some sermon or book that you have read, and you will find some of your smaller notes will come in as additional thoughts or illustrations. In going over these sheets continually they will gradually arrange themselves, so that you should generally have five or six that have got beyond the stage of loose notes, and are showing signs that they will ultimately grow into good sermons. I would put them in the order of their completeness. Those that were fullest and most worked out should be on the top, and I would make a rule, in cases of perplexity, to take my top sheet, that which was the most forward and best worked out, and resolve to put my best into that. I would put all other subjects aside, and waste no more time thinking. You will see that this drawer is for your times of perplexity about a subject. Do not let these times be very frequent. Try to have your sermon plans sketched for some weeks or months to come, so that you know on Monday morning what you intend to preach.

§ 3

Now then, Monday or Tuesday has come, and next Sunday's sermon is before you. Your first business is to choose your text, or to choose your subject. For myself it is usually a subject that I think of, and then I find a text to express what I want to teach. I think that is a very natural thing. At any rate, if you are to preach from a text, be sure you study it carefully, and not apart from its context. Preachers sometimes preach great nonsense from "texts." Ruskin, in his *Ethics of the Dust,* hits off cleverly the way that some men

take their text without its context. He says,
"It is just like the way the old monks thought
that hedgehogs ate grapes. They rolled themselves, it was said, over and over where the
grapes lay on the ground. Whatever stuck to
their spikes they carried off and ate. But,"
he adds, "you can only get the skins of the texts
that way; if you want their juice you must
press them in cluster." Think of the whole
trend of Bible teaching on that subject, not
merely what your text says. Study the context
carefully. Be sure you find out what the writer
really meant who wrote your text.

And in this connection let me say that, except
in expository sermons—which, of course, ex-
pound the whole passage—you will generally
do best by taking one important thought and
hammering it out on every side, and deter-
mining to get that one thought into the minds
of the people. There may be little subordinate
thoughts to be touched in passing as you go on.
But let every sermon be on one subject—one
thought—so that you could write in one sentence, "This is the thought that I want to impress on the people; this is my clear aim; this is
exactly what I want them to feel; or, this is
exactly what I want them to do."

Never write a sermon in which you have not a definite, clear aim. I have heard such sermons carefully prepared and eloquently delivered, too. But I could not see why the man preached them. I could see no purpose in them, except, perhaps, the purpose of preaching a sermon. One would think no man would be such an idiot as to preach without any definite purpose. But I think some do. It is as if a man were working hard with wood and hammer and nails, and when you ask him what he is working at—what he is making—and he should say, "I am not quite clear about it; I am only hammering." That is why I insist on your writing for me at the beginning of every sermon in Hall, writing in one sentence what the man in the pew would say to the man in the street in telling about your sermon.

Never, I say, write a sermon in which it is not perfectly clear to you and to your audience: "This is what I want the people to feel; this is what I want the people to do."

§ 4

Now you have got your subject. What next? I don't know. It depends on the man himself.

Scarcely any two men work the same way. I can give you some hints and show you my own way. I am usually told that the first thing to do is to think out your subject and arrange its separate headings and the line on which it will run. That looks plausible. But for myself I seldom do it. My first effort is to collect material. I never try to arrange it until after I have got it. And such queer and unexpected things come in as material that I never know till the end of my collecting what the heads will be or what exact lines I shall follow.

I do not mean that I start without knowing at all what I shall say. No! I have read somewhere that that is the ideal way to write a love letter, but it certainly is not the best way to write a sermon. You must have some idea of what you want to say, and what you are to aim at. But with myself it is often a bit hazy at first and only clears itself as I go on, like the developing of a photographic plate. I sometimes make my sermon as an artist makes his picture. I fasten on a drawing board a large sheet of paper, the larger the better, usually the large white tea paper, which I can buy in the grocers' shops. First, perhaps, I jot down provisionally the headings that occur to me.

Only provisionally, they will probably alter as I go on. Then, with my big sheet of paper before me, I get my head into my hands and force myself to think hard for an hour or so. Sometimes a good deal comes of this, sometimes very little: generally what comes is most fragmentary and disorderly—a decision as to the way of concluding and enforcing my point, a thought of certain Scriptural passages that bear on it, a choice of one for my text, a memory of thoughts already stored in my mind or experiences in my own life, or of some incidents in the parish, a recollection of some event in history or story that I have read. Hopes, aspirations, enthusiasms, desires, thoughts of many kinds, that come flashing themselves before me in that mysterious way, as if they were living things coming on me at my call from somewhere outside me—suitable thoughts and unsuitable—coming slowly and laboriously or coming rushingly and impetuously, according to the mood that is on me at the time. From these I choose rapidly and jot down instantly, in any order, all over my large white sheet. Then I take down my interleaved Bible and look up my text and the Scripture passages that are similar to it, to see if on the opposite blank page I have noted down any illustrations, or sermons, or references of any kind. These I read up carefully; then I get my common-place book and see if under any of its headings there is anything to help me. Then I stop for the day, with a tired head and a hot flushed face; I have done between two and three hours, it is all I am able for. But the work of this first morning tells. It is the foundation. It is the collecting of germ thoughts, which curiously grow and grow, and weave garments for themselves out of my sick visit and my school teaching, and my letters and my odd reading, and the conversation of the people during my visiting. I talk to people about it if they will let me. You see I have made the subject of that sermon my central thought for the week, and the mind in such cases has a curious trick of grouping everything round that centre and making them adapt themselves to it.

What I have described as my first morning is an exceptionally good one. Very often I leave my study disappointed and worried. My mind was barren, my feelings were dead and cold. All I could do was to read up what others had said on the subject, especially any published sermons that I had bearing in any way on it.

But even that was something. These thoughts of others, though cold and uninspiring as being outside of myself, yet kept the subject before me and made my mind begin to work.

Next day I try again, perhaps not nearly so well. And the odd disconnected jottings on my paper begin to sort themselves out. I see this thought connects itself with that one, and both will come in best in the middle of my sermon. I mark them both G. Here are a set of thoughts and an illustration that will come in best in the beginning; I write a letter A beside each, and so on. Then I tear up my sheet and substitute a new one. This is the canvas for my picture. On this new sheet I write out these jottings, all grouped together in their right connection, and I begin to see now how my sermon will run, and again I get my head into my hands and force my mind to work and brood over the whole. If I have succeeded, the sermon is a stage further on, and the stray thoughts of the rest of the day touch it a little more. Here I add a suggestion which means a good deal to myself. Think with your pen. Instead of working out a thought fully in my mind I take my pen and keep writing as I think. At first it is vague, stupid wording.

But that pen clears and excites thought in a curious way. And sometimes in ten minutes I am writing freely and soon one section of my sermon is done.

§ 5

Now it is time to write out the sermon. This one should do in any case, whether it is to be written or extempore. In the next lecture I shall discuss that question of extempore or written sermons. But I must insist here that extempore preaching, if it is to be real, honest preaching, must take as much time and trouble —probably much more time and trouble—than the written sermon. It should, in most cases, be, at least, roughly written out to clear your thoughts. For extempore delivery you do not need to trouble about the language and the balance of your sentences. But I think you ought to write it out fully, or nearly so, at least for many years to come.

In writing out I used to begin at the beginning, which seems to be the right and logical way. I don't now. I have found by experience that I wasted too much time on the introduction, and found myself tired and cramped for room before I reached the end. I have found, too, that the part which I felt deeply yesterday, I feel less to-day. So now, instead of a nicely sewed manuscript sermon begun on the first page and finished on the last, I write on separate loose sheets.

I write straight off just whatever strikes me most—perhaps the end, perhaps the middle, perhaps some striking story or illustration. My two rules are—(1) Write at once whatever is hottest and most vivid in my mind, whatever can rouse my feelings most at the time; (2) Be much more careful about the end than about the beginning. Don't imagine from this that the introduction is unimportant. It is very important. A good, striking beginning will catch the attention of the people, and, if you are wise and careful in the rest of the sermon, may enable you to hold them to the end. It is very important. But the ending is of vital importance. Lead up to it. Make it the strongest, most incisive part of your sermon.

When I began preaching I used not to announce the heads or divisions of my sermon. It seemed to me stiff and formal and old-fashioned. And, of course, like all young young preachers, I must be original. I have changed my mind about that, as about many other things. I do not formally announce my divisions, but I take great pains to let the audience know them. You must remember that a preached sermon is not like a printed one, where the reader can see the divisions and paragraphs, and where he can look back to the beginning of a passage for the connection. If the audience are not helped in some way to guess at the coming line of thought, they get confused very soon, and you lose their attention.

So much do I feel this that I now usually begin, after announcing my text, by saying— The subject of my sermon to-day will be, etc. Then, when I come to each separate division of my thought, I indicate it clearly by a deliberate pause, or by summing up into a sentence the previous thought. I somehow or other try to put the people into the position of a man who had the sermon and its headings before him. I only want to give you the hint. Try to put them in the position of the reader of the manuscript.

§ 6

There are many more things to be said about preparation, which you must learn for yourselves. Each man must learn what is most fitting for himself.

But there is one thing that I must say in conclusion, since it is true for us all. Your success in preparing a helpful and interesting sermon depends largely on your power of thinking about your audience and putting yourself in their place. You must first have learned a good deal about them and the lives they live—that is one great gain of regular visiting—and then before you write your sermon call them up in imagination before you, as they will be on Sunday when you are preaching. Think about that man with the sceptical temperament, who sits in the front pew. He is not a bad fellow, and does not want to find you wrong, but he will certainly criticise and sift every weak statement. Think of the tempted and the openly careless people. Think of the poor sorrowful hearts that so greatly want comfort, and the earnest strugglers who want to be heartened up, and the loving faithful old Christians, who know far more about God and His love and the daily communion with Him than you do, and yet who listen so humbly that you grow ashamed to be preaching to them. I shall speak to you afterwards of the need of doing this fully when you stand in the pulpit and look into their faces before the sermon and try to realise what a world of thought and will and feeling lies behind each face. But you must first think about them in your study, if the sermon is really to lay hold of them. I frequently spend part of my preparation time in the pulpit in the empty church with my mind peopling the pews as I go on.

Now the sermon is written. Are you done? If it be at all like mine you certainly are not done.[1] The first thing that I usually find is that I have said too much and over-written the number of pages that should make a twenty minutes' sermon. The people will often listen with interest to a sermon of twenty-five or thirty minutes. But it is not safe to risk it. It needs to be a very interesting one, and to have gripped them well. It is much better to let them feel that they could have listened to you longer. I always find my sermon is too

[1] In revising the proofs for press the writer notices on certain pages more mention of himself and his methods than seems to him quite desirable in the publicity of print. It would be difficult now to recast those pages. Will the reader kindly note that these lectures were not intended for publication, and that in the privacy of a lecture hall one might find it desirable, in a subject such as this, to enforce his teaching by frequent reference to his own methods and experience.

long. I always have to cut it down ruthlessly; reduce and condense and cut out altogether part of what I have said. It vexes me, but I think it is good for me, and probably the sermon is the stronger and more vigorous for it. Every sentence that is not accomplishing something must go.

Then you must go over it again and ask, Have I put my main points really well? Are they quite distinct? Don't hesitate, if necessary, to repeat them again and again, but be sure that they are clear and that they get into the people's minds.

Also ask, is the sermon interesting? Does it begin well? Does it end well? Are there any dull pages in it? Have I done my best to relieve the attention repeatedly by introducing an illustration, or by keeping every point clear and lucid? Test your sermon by Cicero's famous rules that I have already mentioned—(1) *Placere;* (2) *Docere;* (3) *Movere.*

(1) *Placere*—To please and interest the audience. Have I interested my audience?

(2) *Docere*—To do this in order to teach them. Have I taught? Have I given definite instruction—not mere empty exhorting and declaiming?

(3) *Movere*—To do the teaching in order to move their hearts. Is my sermon calculated to do that? Would it move me if I heard another man preach it? What did I want to move them to? To do something? or to feel something? or both? Have I succeeded? Could I do it better?

There is more to be said, but it will come in better in the next lecture on "The Preaching of the Sermon."

PREACHING THE SERMON

LECTURE VI

PREACHING THE SERMON

§ 1

WE close now this brief course of lectures. I have to speak to you about "Preaching the Sermon." And I think this is, perhaps, the best place to discuss the very obvious question, Should you aim at preaching written or extempore sermons?

It ought to go without saying that you must certainly write out what you mean to say for your first few years at any rate if you are to escape the fluent talking of twaddle that discredits so many of our pulpits. But after the first few years, should your sermon be written or extempore?

I cannot answer the question for any of you. No man can answer it for you: it depends entirely on yourself. There are, I think, some men who should never attempt to preach extempore. There are many men, on the other hand, who quite spoil the effect of their preaching by writing, and reading from a manuscript; and there are others, and I think these the greatest number, who, by sometimes preaching extempore, would increase their power of clear and vigorous writing, and who, by sometimes carefully writing out their sermons, would increase the accuracy of their extempore speaking. I do not see at all why any man should confine himself to either method exclusively. But I do not see, either, why any man should adopt the method that does not suit him; why he should be a dull reader of manuscript if he has the power of quick, alert, vigorous speech; or why he should be a stupid extempore ranter of commonplaces, when God, who has denied him the alert nimbleness of thought, has given him the ability to write careful, well-thought-out sermons. There is no particular virtue in either manuscript or extempore. Preach in the way you can do best; only be quite sure that it is because you can do it best that way, not because it is easier and lazier to do it that way. Each method has its own advantages and defects.

§ 2

There is a great deal to say in favour of extempore preaching. In fact, to the man who is capable of doing it really well there is no question but that it is the better way. But, then, it should be the true sort of extempore preaching. It should require, if anything, harder work and more careful study than the written sermon. Extempore speaking should never mean speaking without careful preparation; it should never mean that the preacher does not know beforehand what he is going to say. It should mean that he knows right well what he is going to say, but does not know exactly in what words he will say it.

Rightly understood, it is a real, direct speaking by man to men. The personality of the preacher is not obscured by the intervention of a manuscript. I do not want to overestimate its importance. There is a tendency to do this amongst the less thoughtful in our congregations. They attach the idea of piety and faith and dependence on God to extempore preaching as contrasted with written sermons. I remember, in my early ministry, a dear old lady friend who was looking forward to the day when I should have the courage and faith to fling aside my manuscript and trust myself fully on the promises of Christ—"Settle it therefore in your hearts not to meditate before what ye shall answer, for I will give you a mouth and wisdom." It was not easy to explain to her that that promise was not made to a lazy young preacher to save him preparation of his sermon, but to men in danger of their lives when they should be dragged before councils for His sake. I hope you will keep this fact clearly in mind when you are tempted to be lazy in your preparation. Do not let any one persuade you that there is a word of promise for any man who wants to attain results without working for them. But though I know that part of the preference for extempore preaching arises from false notions of the meaning of Scripture, yet I know, too, that is not the whole reason of it. The people feel that it is more direct speaking to them. There is a quickness and liveliness and spontaneous flow of feeling that they usually miss in the read manuscript sermon. And to the speaker himself there is a delight and excitement in the extempore discourse that is very much missing in the other.

I say all this, though I seldom preach really

extempore myself. I wish I could do it, and do it well. I know it would bring more effectiveness, and I know it would bring more enjoyment to myself in preaching. But I have thought the matter carefully out for many years, and I feel that I must recognise my limitations. I am not easy and self-possessed enough to "let myself go," without risk of saying the wrong thing. When I grow intensely interested in my subject, and the thoughts are coming faster than I can overtake them, I find I lack the nimbleness and alertness of brain to choose my words quickly and correctly. I have repeatedly regretted my extempore sermon.

I still say I wish I could preach extempore. I still say to you, "preach extempore if you really can do it best." But I warn you that there are dangers connected with so doing, and you need to be a high type of man, morally as well as intellectually, to avoid those dangers. So many extempore preachers that I know seem to me to have grown very lazy. They seem to content themselves with sketching out the line of thought, the bare headings of the sermons, and trust to the excitement of the preaching and the inspiration that comes from a listening crowd to supply the words. I know a few extempore preachers whose thought is as clear and deliberate and logically put as if every word of it were written. I feel they must have worked very hard at their preparation. But I fear many of the extempore preachers that I know are poor preachers, and show much trace of habits of loose, inexact thought and lazy and hurried preparation. Such preaching is very easy and very useless. Archbishop Whately used to say it reminded him of Bottom's answer in the play when Snug, the joiner, asked if the lion's part was yet written —"No, it can be done extempore, for it is only roaring."

In a word, you will be a much better and more effective preacher if you can preach well extempore, and if you can trust yourself, by God's grace, to surmount the temptation to laziness in preparing. But you must recognise that there are grave dangers to be guarded against.

§ 3

On the other hand, the written sermon has also its advantages and disadvantages. It does much to secure deliberate thinking, steady industry, exact careful expression of thought.

It keeps you from running off into fluent verbosity and well-sounding nothings which the presence of an audience sometimes induces. It has two other advantages which I have seldom heard spoken of. One is what I greatly feel myself, the freedom from strain and anxiety all through the previous service in church. When I have to speak without a written sermon I suffer a good deal beforehand. I try not to be irreverent, and not to let my thoughts through the prayers run on to the sermon. But I seldom succeed, and, in any case, it is a great strain on me. I dare say it is with me a matter of temperament, and of being unaccustomed to much extempore speaking. But I think most men would feel the strain in some degree.

And the other advantage I refer to is that in holiday time, or in times of severe pressure of other work, you have a carefully written old sermon to fall back upon. I certainly do not want to encourage any laziness in preachers. I have no love for old sermons; they never have the freshness and spontaneity that they had at first; but in the strain of a busy life they are at times a great help and rest. I think there is a great deal of silly thought and talk in the objection to preaching old sermons. A preacher

has written some sermons that have cost him
weeks of thinking, and on subjects that he
thinks very much need to be preached on. He
has expressed himself better than he could do
if he were to try it again. Why on earth he
should not repeat that sermon and throw his
whole heart into it I cannot see. Why he
should be ashamed to confess that he had
preached it before I cannot see either. Of
course, I see the danger here—the same temptation to laziness that I pointed out in the extempore sermon. But the abuse of a practice
does not forbid the legitimate use of it. And,
certainly, in the holiday times, or in the pressure of new and unaccustomed work, no man
need hesitate to lay his old sermon down before
God and beseech His blessing on it as if it were
a new one.

These are the advantages of the written sermon. But, alas! they are frequently more than
balanced by its disadvantages. In six cases out
of ten the written sermon stands as a screen
between the souls of the preacher and people.
So many men *read* their written sermons—
literally READ them as if they were the work of
some one else; as if their own personality were
not in them at all. It is pitiful to see a clergy-

man with his head down and his eyes on the
paper laboriously reading his sermon as if he
had never taken in the thoughts and made them
his own. That is not preaching. And unless
you are afflicted with some constitutional in-
firmity or awkwardness I do not think there is
any excuse for such preaching as that.

§ 4

But I do not think you need be either a fluent
ranter or a stupid reader. I think it is quite
possible to gain all the advantages of the written sermon with only a very small part of its
disadvantages. Some of our greatest preachers—such men as Liddon and Guthrie—have
done so. It depends on how the sermon is prepared and how the sermon is preached. If in
preparing your written sermon you have really
put yourself into it, thought its thoughts, felt
its feelings, that will show in the delivery of it.
If you have prepared it with the thought of the
people vividly in your mind, it can become
almost like an extempore sermon. Some men
can so write and so think themselves into the
Sunday position that in the quiet study they
feel their faces flushing with the excitement of

it. When that happens you may be sure the sermon will not seem like a written one on Sunday.

But that is not enough. If you are only capable of preaching written sermons you must try all you can to do away with the defects of writing. Make yourself familiar with the manuscript, mark its headings and important passages with coloured pencil so that you shall be able when preaching to look at the people. Then go into the pulpit on Saturday night in the empty church and try to preach your sermon, peopling the pews in your imagination. Learn to express your thought a little differently. Break up your carefully composed sentences into shorter and rougher ones if that is more like your natural style in speaking to the people. You need not rewrite the sentences, simply think whether you can express your thought more easily and naturally. If you will only take trouble enough, I can assure you that your written sermon will gain much of the advantages of extempore speaking, and the people will hardly notice whether you have a manuscript at all. This is quite a different thing from memorizing your sermon and saying it off by heart, which I think tends to unreality and is a custom to be deprecated.

§ 5

Now you are in the pulpit on Sunday, facing your people. If you have not done your best for them you should face them with trouble and shame. But if you have done your best lift up your heart to God and fear not the face of men. You are an ambassador for God. If you have anything worth while saying say it for them and forget all about yourself. In your layman days you have heard so much criticism and condemnation of preachers— more shame for the preachers who have deserved it—that you are probably afraid of the same fate yourself, and it makes you nervous. Do not be afraid. Do not be nervous. All the best of your people will instinctively find out if you have any help for them, and even if you have not much, still they will find out that you wanted to help. And the kindliest critics in the world are the good, earnest Christians who believe that their pastor is in earnest and desirous to help however stupid he may be.

As for the mere "critical layman" in the pew

who is always criticising and "never can understand why clergy are so incompetent," do not trouble too much about him. He is probably not such a very brilliant person himself. He is always expecting far more than he has any right to expect. "Why do we get so many stupid clergy?" one of these gentlemen once asked of Archbishop Temple. "Because, Sir, we have to take them out of the laity," was the prompt retort. That is so. We clergy are, at least, quite average specimens of the layman order from which we come. Try your critic at making a speech. Try even a trained speaker or writer. Compare the average lawyer or journalist with the average preacher. The advantage is not by any means, I think, on the layman's side.

Fear not the face of *men,* I say. But fear the face of *man.* Study to acquire a deep reverence for your congregation. No man ever became a great preacher who did not view with reverence and awe the mysterious immortal beings gathered before him—each one an "I," an "ego," a "self," hiding behind their faces as behind a mask, looking out at him through the windows of their eyes, receiving his thoughts through the portals of their ears—a living spiritual being, an heir of the eternities who is cased up in these changing bodies, who has survived perhaps half a dozen bodies already, and who is destined to survive everything in the Universe except God alone. It is a tremendous thing to realise what beings, what destinies you have to deal with as you stand in that pulpit, speaking your poor stammering words in the name of the Lord. The more you get that deep reverence for the immortal souls before you, the more will you be free from all petty fears of critics or petty thoughts about your own eloquence or cleverness, and the more, too, will you have the courage to resist their prejudices and bigotries when it is necessary, and to preach them what is the need of these immortal souls, the whole wide counsel of God.

§ 6

In your reverence for them realise that at bottom there is the better nature in every one of them, capable of responding to your highest appeals. I feel that strongly. Believe in your people. They may be careless, sinful, hostile to certain views of religion that do not appeal to them, but at bottom, they do not want to be bad. They do want to be helped. The very worst has his better moments of dissatisfaction and vague desire for higher things.

I do not make light of the evil in human nature, but I think there is a good deal of exaggeration and a good deal of cant in the talk about men's hostility to Christ. I do not believe that any men are really hostile to Christ. They may be hostile to your way or my way of presenting Christ. They may have grown so hardened and careless that Christ does not get a fair chance with them. But I think it is true of almost every one of the people who come to your church on Sunday, that they do really care to be good, though they may not take much trouble about it; that if Christ were more truly lifted up He would draw them more surely unto Him.

Oh, I do believe that one great secret of successful preaching is to believe in the better nature of those you are addressing. Believe that they will listen if you make it worth their while to listen. Believe that every one of them has a soft spot in his heart if you can only find it. Believe that in all your enthusiasm for the high, unselfish life you have the sympathy of almost every one of them.

I think that was, humanly speaking, the secret of our Lord's power with the poor publicans and sinners of Jerusalem. He thought the best of them, He looked for the best in them, He hoped the best of them, and therefore, the best in them responded to Him. I think that will be a great source of power with you, too. It is not scolding and faultfinding that will help people. What they want is to be encouraged, to be heartened up, to be made to realise how much of God's grace is given to the very worst of them.

§7

Now your preaching will be much influenced by your realising these things when you stand in the pulpit. Get into the pulpit in time to realise it, not just in the last verse of the hymn. Get time to stand for a few minutes looking into the faces of the people and thinking about them and about the God in whose presence you and they are.

I advise you to let your effort at realising your position run like this:—

(1) I am Christ's appointed messenger to this people to-day. He is present looking and

listening. He is deeply solicitous that these poor strugglers should be helped by me, unworthy though I am. He has given me the supreme privilege and responsibility of being His messenger to them. He will help me. He will not be hard on me. He will make all allowance for me. But, oh, I must try not to disappoint Him.

Let that be your first thought. It will help to sweep away all thought of self. "Am I preaching well? Am I gaining credit for myself?" It will keep you rather asking, "Am I saying anything likely to help any human soul before me? Am I pleasing, or am I displeasing Christ?"

(2) And let this be your second thought—deep sympathy for, and desire to help, the poor strugglers before you. Behind these upturned faces there are hearts and feelings and sorrows and desires and dissatisfactions. Some of them have hard lives, some have severe temptations, some have grown hard and careless and forgetful of God. Try to realise this. I think you might well get the habit here of repeating to yourself as you look at them from the pulpit—

"Lord, some are sick and some are sad,
    And some have never loved Thee well,
And some have lost the love they had,
    And some have found the world in vain,
Yet from the world they break not free,
    And some have friends who give them pain,
Yet have not sought a friend in Thee,
    And none, O Lord, have perfect rest."

Get the habit of repeating these words as you
look slowly into the faces of the people before
you preach. It will rouse your sympathy with
them. It will influence the whole tone of your
sermon.

§ 8

And because the people are so important and
so well worthy of your best, surely you will not
try to preach to them "clever sermons," or
"eloquent sermons." I trust your sermons will
often be both clever and eloquent. But I beseech you do not aim at making them so. Your
business is simply to do your level best to get
your message into the people's heads and
hearts. Your business is to preach Christ and
to keep yourself and your cleverness and eloquence in the background. There is a well
known story of an old painter who had finished
a picture of the Last Supper, and asked a com-

rade painter for his criticism. "That chalice is simply perfect," said his friend. Immediately the painter dashed his brush across it. "Then it is a defect in the picture," he said; "it is drawing attention from the central figure of the Christ."

Watch that yourself never detracts attention from your Lord. Distrust your fine sentences, your bits of eloquence that you are so pleased with. They may be all right, but take care of them. And snub any man who talks to you of the cleverness and eloquence of your sermon. That praise is insulting. You will get some praise that you may take with a glad heart when you get it, and thank God for it. You will get it none too often—when some poor struggler tells you shyly during the week, "I have been trying to do what you suggested last Sunday," or, "It has been a bit easier to fight through this week because of what you said in your sermon." I wish the people would tell us that a little oftener, for I think we do help them oftener than we know. But we seldom get the encouragement of hearing it.

§9

One thing more. Try to acquire the power of keeping in touch with your audience, keeping your finger on their pulse, as it were, so that you will feel conscious when you are interesting and when you are boring them, and when they have had as much of the sermon as they care to listen to. This is a good deal a matter of temperament and sympathy. If you have the orator's instinct you will feel this without any trouble. If you have not, you can at least acquire it partially—by observation. There are many preachers who feel instinctively what points are telling with the audience and what parts are tiring them. There is also a psychological moment when the audience, or most of them, have had just enough. They have not yet begun to tire, but they will in a few moments. Do not let them have those few moments. Draw to a close as quickly as you can. End off abruptly if necessary. Do not let them tire if you can possibly help it. Use every right device to keep their interest for the full time that you want it. But do not go on after you have lost it.

141

This is a hard task I am setting you. Some of you may not be able for it till you have had years of experience. Some of you can instinctively do it from the first. But you must every one of you aim at it. You must not detain your audience when their interest is lost. It will often vex and disappoint you if you follow that rule. Never mind. It will pay in the long-run. They will come to listen to you with fresh interest next time. If you have tired them a few times they will expect to be tired again, and will either stay away or give you half their attention.

The consciousness of this, too, will affect your preparation. You will know that there is danger of losing their attention, and that you will have to use all your guile to put your points in the most interesting way. You will write, or otherwise prepare with the consciousness upon you that there is little use in preaching if the people are not listening.

And here, too, as I said to you in a previous lecture, if you can have the help of a wise, judicious, candid friend, use it freely. Ask him to criticise you. Ask him what points were interesting and where you lost the attention, or whether you stopped up sharply enough to escape doing so. It is not easy to get a friend who can act this part for you. A man's wife—if ever you get a wife—ought to be the best help, unless she is silly enough to think her husband is perfection. There is probably no one else in the congregation who would be more sensitive for you if she is wise enough to see you are imperfect and need helping, and if she is enough in sympathy with your deep desire to do your very best to help the people in your sermon.

Now I have done. All that I have said may be roughly summed up in this. If you are a real man, if you are faithful to your God, if you are honestly trying to do your best, you cannot fail in being, at any rate, a good helpful preacher.

THE END